Palo Alto Networks Certified Network Security Engineer on PAN-OS 7 (PCNSE7) Exam Practice Questions & Dumps

Exam Practice Questions For Palo Alto Networks PAN-OS 7 (PCNSE7) Exam Prep LATEST VERSION

PRESENTED BY: Quantic Books

About Quantic Books:

Quantic Books is a publishing house based in Princeton, New Jersey, USA. , a platform that is accessible online as well as locally, which gives power to educational content, erudite collection, poetry & many other book genres. We make it easy for writers & authors to get their books designed, published, promoted, and sell professionally on worldwide scale with eBook + Print distribution. Quantic Books is now distributing books worldwide.

Note: Find answers of the questions at the last of the book.

QUESTION 1

Which Public Key infrastructure factor is used to authorize users for GlobalProtect when the Connect Procedure is set to pre-logon?

A. Certificate revocation list

B. Trusted root certificate

C. Machine certificate

D. Online Certificate Status Protocol

QUESTION 2

What can absent SSL packets when doing a packet capture on dataplane interfaces?

A. The packets are hardware offloaded to the offloaded processor on the dataplane

B. The absent packets are offloaded to the management plane CPU

C. The packets are not captured for the reason that they are encrypted

D. There is a hardware problem with offloading FPGA on the management plane

QUESTION 3

A corporation has a web server behind a Palo Alto Networks next-generation firewall that it wants to make accessible to the public at 1.1.1.1. The corporation has resolved to organize a destination NAT Policy guideline.

Given the following zone information:

· DMZ zone: DMZ-L3

· Public zone: Untrust-L3

· Guest zone: Guest-L3

· Web server zone: Trust-L3

· Public IP address (Untrust-L3): 1.1.1.1

· Private IP address (Trust-L3): 192.168.1.50

What must be organized as the destination zone on the Original Packet tab of NAT Policy guideline?

A. Untrust-L3
B. DMZ-L3
C. Guest-L3
D. Trust-L3

QUESTION 4

A host added to ethernet1/3 cannot access the internet. The default gateway is added to ethernet1/4. After troubleshooting. It is decided that traffic cannot pass from the ethernet1/3 to ethernet1/4. What can be the reason of the problem?

A. DHCP has been set to Auto.
B. Interface ethernet1/3 is in Layer 2 mode and interface ethernet1/4 is in Layer 3 mode.
C. Interface ethernet1/3 and ethernet1/4 are in Virtual Wire Mode.
D. DNS has not been precisely organized on the firewall

QUESTION 5

What are three effective actions in a File Blocking Profile? (Select three)

A. Forward
B. Block
C. Alert
D. Upload
E. Reset-both
F. Continue

QUESTION 6

Which customer software can be used to connect remote Linux customer into a Palo Alto Networks Infrastructure without sacrificing the ability to scan traffic and protect in contrast to risks?

A. X-Auth IPsec VPN
B. GlobalProtect Apple IOS
C. GlobalProtect SSL
D. GlobalProtect Linux

QUESTION 7

A customer is deploying a pair of PA-5000 series firewalls using High Availability (HA) in Active/Passive mode. Which report is accurate about this deployment?

A. The two devices needs to share a routable floating IP address
B. The two devices may be different models within the PA-5000 series
C. The HA1 IP address from each peer needs to be on a different subnet
D. The management port may be used for a backup control connection

QUESTION 8

How is the Forward Untrust Certificate used?

A. It problems certificates encountered on the Untrust security zone when customers attempt to connect to a site that has be decrypted/
B. It is used when web servers request a customer certificate.
C. It is presented to customers when the server they are connecting to is signed by a certificate authority that is not trusted by firewall.
D. It is used for Captive Portal to identify unknown users.

QUESTION 9

A corporation is upgrading its existing Palo Alto Networks firewall from version 7.0.1 to 7.0.4.

Which three procedures can the firewall manager use to install PAN-OS 7.0.4 across the enterprise? (Select three)

A. Download PAN-OS 7.0.4 files from the support site and install them on each firewall after manually uploading.
B. Download PAN-OS 7.0.4 to a USB drive and the firewall will automatically update after the USB drive is inserted in the firewall.
C. Push the PAN-OS 7.0.4 updates from the support site to install on each firewall.
D. Push the PAN-OS 7.0.4 update from one firewall to all of the other remaining after updating one firewall.
E. Download and install PAN-OS 7.0.4 directly on each firewall.
F. Download and push PAN-OS 7.0.4 from Panorama to each firewall.

QUESTION 10

A network security engineer is asked to perform a Return Merchandise Authorization (RMA) on a firewall

Which part of files needs to be imported back into the replacement firewall that is using Panorama?

A. Device state and license files
B. Configuration and serial number files
C. Configuration and statistics files
D. Configuration and Large Scale VPN (LSVPN) setups file

QUESTION 11

N NO: 56

A firewall manager is troubleshooting problems with traffic passing through the Palo Alto Networks firewall. Which procedure shows the global counters related with the traffic after configuring the suitable packet filters?

A. From the CLI, problem the show counter global filter pcap yes command.
B. From the CLI, problem the show counter global filter packet-filter yes command.
C. From the GUI, select show global counters under the monitor tab.
D. From the CLI, problem the show counter interface command for the ingress interface.

QUESTION 12

Corporation.com has an in-house application that the Palo Alto Networks device doesn't identify precisely. A Threat Management Team member has mentioned that this in-house application is very sensitive and all traffic being identified needs to be inspected by the Content-ID engine.

Which procedure must corporation.com use to directly address this traffic on a Palo Alto Networks device?

A. Make a custom Application without signatures, then make an Application Override policy that includes the source, Destination, Destination Port/Protocol and Custom Application of the traffic.
B. Wait until an official Application signature is delivered from Palo Alto Networks.
C. Modify the session timer settings on the closest referenced application to meet the needs of the in-house application
D. Make a Custom Application with signatures matching unique identifiers of the in-house application traffic

QUESTION 13

A dangerous US-CERT notification is published regarding a newly discovered botnet. The malware is very evasive and is not reliably detected by endpoint antivirus software. Furthermore, SSL is used to tunnel malicious traffic to command-and-control servers on the internet and SSL Forward Proxy Decryption is not enabled.

Which factor once enabled on a perimeter firewall will allow the identification of existing infected hosts in an environment?

A. Anti-Spyware profiles applied outbound security policies with DNS Query action set to sinkhole
B. File Blocking profiles applied to outbound security policies with action set to alert
C. Vulnerability Protection profiles applied to outbound security policies with action set to block
D. Antivirus profiles applied to outbound security policies with action set to alert

QUESTION 14

A Palo Alto Networks firewall is being targeted by an NTP Amplification attack and is being flooded with tens thousands of bogus UDP connections per second to a single destination IP address and post.

Which option when enabled with the correction threshold would mitigate this attack without dropping legitirnate traffic to other hosts insides the network?

A. Zone Protection Policy with UDP Flood Protection
B. QoS Policy to throttle traffic below maximum limit
C. Security Policy guideline to deny traffic to the IP address and port that is under attack
D. Classified DoS Protection Policy using destination IP only with a Protect action

QUESTION 15

Which three purpose are found on the dataplane of a PA-5050? (Select three)

A. Protocol Decoder
B. Dynamic routing
C. Management
D. Network Processing
E. Signature Match

QUESTION 16

Which Palo Alto Networks VM-Series firewall is supported for VMware NSX?

A. VM-100
B. VM-200
C. VM-1000-HV
D. VM-300

QUESTION 17

What are three effective procedure of user mapping? (Select three)

A. Syslog
B. XML API
C. 802.1X
D. WildFire
E. Server Monitoring

QUESTION 18

Which three log-forwarding destinations require a server profile to be organized? (Select three)

A. SNMP Trap
B. Email
C. RADIUS
D. Kerberos
E. Panorama
F. Syslog

QUESTION 19

Which command can be used to authorize a Captive Portal policy?

A. eval captive-portal policy <criteria>
B. request cp-policy-eval <criteria>
C. test cp-policy-match <criteria>
D. debug cp-policy <criteria>

QUESTION 20

How does Panorama handle incoming logs when it reaches the maximum storage capacity?

A. Panorama discards incoming logs when storage capacity full.

B. Panorama stops accepting logs until licenses for additional storage space are applied

C. Panorama stops accepting logs until a reboot to clean storage space.

D. Panorama automatically deletes older logs to make space for new ones.

QUESTION 21

A network security engineer has been asked to analyze Wildfire activity. However, the Wildfire Submissions item is not visible form the Monitor tab.

What could reason this condition?

A. The firewall does not have an active WildFire subscription.

B. The engineer's account does not have permission to view WildFire Submissions.

C. A policy is blocking WildFire Submission traffic.

D. Though WildFire is working, there are currently no WildFire Submissions log entries.

QUESTION 22

Which two procedures can be used to mitigate resource exhaustion of an application server? (Select two)

A. Vulnerability Object
B. DoS Protection Profile
C. Data Filtering Profile
D. Zone Protection Profile

QUESTION 23

Only two Trust to Untrust allow guidelines have been made in

the Security policy Guideline1 allows google-base

Guideline2 allows youtube-base

The youtube-base App-ID depends on google-base to purpose. The google-base App-ID implicitly uses SSL and web-browsing. When user try to accesss https://www.youtube.com in a web browser, they get an error indecating that the server cannot be found.

Which action will allow youtube.com display in the browser precisely?

A. Add SSL App-ID to Guideline1
B. Make an additional Trust to Untrust Guideline, add the web-browsing, and SSL App-ID's to it
C. Add the DNS App-ID to Guideline2
D. Add the Web-browsing App-ID to Guideline2

QUESTION 24

Which two mechanisms help prevent a spilt brain scenario an Active/Passive High Availability (HA) pair? (Select two)

A. Organize the management interface as HA3 Backup
B. Organize Ethernet 1/1 as HA1 Backup

Organize Ethernet 1/1 as HA2 Backup
C. Organize the management interface as HA2 Backup
D. Organize the management interface as HA1 Backup
E. Organize ethernet1/1 as HA3 Backup

QUESTION 25

The corporation's Panorama server (IP 10.10.10.5) is not able to manage a firewall that was recently deployed. The firewall's dedicated management port is being used to connect to the management network.

Which two commands may be used to troubleshoot this problem from the CLI of the new firewall? (Select two)

A. test panoramas-connect 10.10.10.5
B. show panoramas-status
C. show arp all I match 10.10.10.5
D. topdump filter "host 10.10.10.5
E. debug data plane packet-diag set capture on

QUESTION 26

A corporation has a policy that denies all applications it classifies as bad and permits only application it classifies as good. The firewall manager made the following security policy on the corporation's firewall.

Which interface configuration will accept specific VLAN IDs?

Which two benefits are gained from having both guideline 2 and guideline 3 presents? (select two)

A. A report can be made that identifies unclassified traffic on the network.
B. Different security profiles can be applied to traffic matching guidelines 2 and 3.
C. Guideline 2 and 3 apply to traffic on different ports.
D. Separate Log Forwarding profiles can be applied to guidelines 2 and 3.

QUESTION 27

A logging infrastructure may need to handle more than 10,000 logs per second. Which two options support a dedicated log collector purpose? (Select two)
A. Panorama virtual appliance on ESX(i) only
B. M-500
C. M-100 with Panorama installed
D. M-100

QUESTION 28

Click the Exhibit button below,

A firewall has three PBF guidelines and a default route with a

Name	Tags	Zone/Interface	Source Address	User	Destination Address	Application
1 PBF1	none	Trust-L3	192.168.10.0/24	any	172.16.10.0/24	any
2 PBF2	none	Trust-L3	192.168.10.0/24	any	172.16.10.0/24	any
3 PBF3	none	Trust-L3	192.168.10.0/24	Will	172.16.10.0/24	any

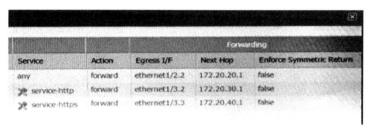

Service	Action	Egress I/F	Forwarding Next Hop	Enforce Symmetric Return
any	forward	ethernet1/2.2	172.20.20.1	false
service-http	forward	ethernet1/3.2	172.20.30.1	false
service-https	forward	ethernet1/3.3	172.20.40.1	false

next hop of 172.20.10.1 that is

organized in the default VR. A user named Will has a PC with a 192.168.10.10 IP address. He makes an HTTPS connection to 172.16.10.20.

Which is the next hop IP address for the HTTPS traffic from

Will's PC? A. 172.20.30.1
B. 172.20.40.1
C. 172.20.20.1
D. 172.20.10.1

QUESTION 29

Which three options are available when creating a security profile? (Select three)

A. Anti-Malware
B. File Blocking
C. Url Filtering
D. IDS/ISP
E. Threat Prevention
F. Antivirus

QUESTION 30

After pushing a security policy from Panorama to a PA-3020 firewall, the firewall manager notices that traffic logs from the PA-3020 are not appearing in Panorama's traffic logs. What could be the problem?

A. A Server Profile has not been organized for logging to this Panorama device.
B. Panorama is not licensed to receive logs from this particular firewall.
C. The firewall is not licensed for logging to this Panorama device.
D. None of the firewall's policies have been assigned a Log Forwarding profile

QUESTION 31

A network Manager needs to view the default action for a specific spyware signature. The manager follows the tabs and menus through Objects> Security Profiles> Anti- Spyware and select default profile.

What must be done next?

A. Click the simple-critical guideline and then click the Action drop-down list.
B. Click the Exceptions tab and then click show all signatures.
C. View the default actions displayed in the Action column.
D. Click the Guidelines tab and then look for guidelines with "default" in the Action column.

QUESTION 32

The web server is organized to listen for HTTP traffic on port 8080. The customers access the web server using the IP address 1.1.1.100 on TCP Port 80. The destination NAT guideline is organized to translate both IP address and report to 10.1.1.100 on TCP Port 8080.

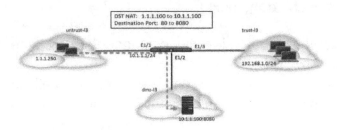

Which NAT and security guidelines needs to be organized on the firewall? (Select two)

A. A security policy with a source of any from untrust-l3 Zone to a destination of 10.1.1.100 in dmz-l3 zone using web-browsing application

B. A NAT guideline with a source of any from untrust-l3 zone to a destination of 10.1.1.100 in dmz-zone using service-http service.

C. A NAT guideline with a source of any from untrust-l3 zone to a destination of 1.1.1.100 in untrust-l3 zone using service-http service.

D. A security policy with a source of any from untrust-l3 zone to a destination of 1.1.100 in dmz-l3 zone using web-browsing application.

QUESTION 33

What are three possible verdicts that WildFire can provide for an analyzed sample? (Select three)

A. Clean
B. Benign
C. Adware
D. Suspicious
E. Grayware
F. Malware

QUESTION 34

A VPN connection is set up between Site-A and Site-B, but no traffic is passing in the system log of Site-A, there is an event logged as like-nego-p1-fail-psk.

What action will bring the VPN up and allow traffic to start passing between the sites?

A. Change the Site-B IKE Gateway profile version to match Site-A,
B. Change the Site-A IKE Gateway profile exchange mode to aggressive mode.
C. Enable NAT Traversal on the Site-A IKE Gateway profile.
D. Change the pre-shared key of Site-B to match the pre-shared key of Site-A

QUESTION 35

Which Security Policy Guideline configuration option disables antivirus and anti-spyware scanning of server-to-customer flows only?

A. Disable Server Response Inspection
B. Apply an Application Override
C. Disable HIP Profile
D. Add server IP Security Policy exception

QUESTION 36

How are IPV6 DNS queries organized to user interface ethernet1/3?

A. Network > Virtual Router > DNS Interface
B. Objects > Customer Objects > DNS
C. Network > Interface Mgrnt
D. Device > Setup > Services > Service Route Configuration

QUESTION 37

What needs to be used in Security Policy Guideline that contain addresses where NAT policy applies?

A. Pre-NAT addresses and Pre-NAT zones
B. Post-NAT addresses and Post-Nat zones
C. Pre-NAT addresses and Post-Nat zones
D. Post-Nat addresses and Pre-NAT zones

QUESTION 38

Palo Alto Networks maintains a dynamic database of malicious domains.

Which two Security Platform factors use this database to prevent risks? (Select two)

A. Brute-force signatures
B. BrightCloud Url Filtering
C. PAN-DB URL Filtering
D. DNS-based command-and-control signatures

QUESTION 39

A network manager uses Panorama to push security polices to managed firewalls at branch offices. Which policy type must be organized on Panorama if the managers at the branch office sites to override these products?

A. Pre-Guidelines
B. Post Guidelines
C. Explicit Guidelines
D. Implicit Guidelines

QUESTION 40

Site-A and Site-B have a site-to-site VPN set up between them. OSPF is organized to dynamically make the routes between the sites. The OSPF configuration in Site-A is organized precisely, but the route for the tunner is not being established. The Site-B interfaces in the graphic are using a broadcast Link Type. The manager has decided that the OSPF configuration in Site-B is using the wrong Link Type for one of its interfaces.

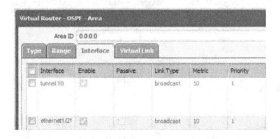

Which Link Type setting will precise the error?

A. Set tunnel. 1 to p2p
B. Set tunnel. 1 to p2mp
C. Set Ethernet 1/1 to p2mp
D. Set Ethernet 1/1 to p2p

QUESTION 41

Which two interface types can be used when configuring Global Protect Portal? (Select two)

A. Virtual Wire
B. Loopback
C. Layer 3
D. Tunnel

QUESTION 42

The GlobalProtect Portal interface and IP address have been organized. Which other value needs to be defined to complete the network settings configuration of GlobalPortect Portal?

A. Server Certificate
B. Customer Certificate
C. Authentication Profile
D. Certificate Profile

QUESTION 43

A network engineer has revived a report of problems reaching 98.139.183.24 through vr1 on the firewall. The routing table on this firewall is extensive and complex.

Which CLI command will help identify the problem?

A. test routing fib virtual-router vr1
B. show routing route type static destination 98.139.183.24
C. test routing fib-lookup ip 98.139.183.24 virtual-router vr1
D. show routing interface

QUESTION 44

Which two options are required on an M-100 appliance to organize it as a Log Collector? (Select two)

A. From the Panorama tab of the Panorama GUI select Log Collector mode and then commit changes
B. Enter the command request system system-mode logger then enter Y to confirm the change to Log Collector mode.
C. From the Device tab of the Panorama GUI select Log Collector mode and then commit changes.
D. Enter the command logger-mode enable the enter Y to confirm the change to Log Collector mode.
E. Log in the Panorama CLI of the dedicated Log Collector

QUESTION 45

Which interface configuration will accept specific VLAN IDs?

A. Tab Mode
B. Sub interface
C. Access Interface
D. Trunk Interface

QUESTION 46

A corporation has a pair of Palo Alto Networks firewalls organized as an Acitve/Passive High Availability (HA) pair.

What allows the firewall manager to determine the last date a failover event occurred?

A. From the CLI problem use the show System log
B. Apply the filter subtype eq ha to the System log
C. Apply the filter subtype eq ha to the configuration log
D. Check the status of the High Availability widget on the Dashboard of the GUI

QUESTION 47

Which three options does the WF-500 appliance support for local analysis? (Select three)

A. E-mail links
B. APK files
C. jar files
D. PNG files
E. Portable Executable (PE) files

QUESTION 48

A host added to Ethernet 1/4 cannot ping the default gateway. The widget on the dashboard shows Ethernet 1/1 and Ethernet 1/4 to be green. The IP address of Ethernet 1/1 is 192.168.1.7 and the IP address of Ethernet 1/4 is 10.1.1.7. The default gateway is added to Ethernet 1/1. A default route is precisely organized.

What can be the reason of this problem?

A. No Zone has been organized on Ethernet 1/4.
B. Interface Ethernet 1/1 is in Virtual Wire Mode.
C. DNS has not been precisely organized on the firewall.
D. DNS has not been precisely organized on the host.

QUESTION 49

Which three fields can be included in a pcap filter? (Select three)

A. Egress interface
B. Source IP
C. Guideline number
D. Destination IP
E. Ingress interface

ANSWERS

1. Correct Answer: C
2. Correct Answer: A
3. Correct Answer: A
4. Correct Answer: B
5. Correct Answer: ABC

Explanation: https://live.paloaltonetworks.com/t5/Configuration-Articles/File-Blocking- Rulebase-and-Action-Precedence/ta-p/53623

6. Correct Answer: D

Explanation:

(http://blog.webernetz.net/2014/03/31/palo-alto-globalprotect-for-linux-with-vpnc/)

7. Correct Answer: D
8. Correct Answer: A
9. Correct Answer: ADF
10. Correct Answer: B
11. Correct Answer: B
12. Correct Answer: A
13. Correct Answer: C
14. Correct Answer: D
15. Correct Answer: BDE
16. Correct Answer: C
17. Correct Answer: BC
18. Correct Answer: ABF
19. Correct Answer: C
20. Correct Answer: D

Explanation:

(https://www.paloaltonetworks.com/documentation/60/panorama/panorama_adminguide/se t-up-panorama/determine-panorama-log-storage-requirements)

21. Correct Answer: A
22. Correct Answer: BD
23. Correct Answer: C
24. Correct Answer: BE
25. Correct Answer: AC
26. Correct Answer: AB
27. Correct Answer: AC

Explanation:

(https://live.paloaltonetworks.com/t5/Management-Articles/Panorama-Sizing-and-Design- Guide/ta-p/72181)

28. Correct Answer: B
29. Correct Answer: BCF
30. Correct Answer: D
31. Correct Answer: B
32. Correct Answer: BD
33. Correct Answer: BEF

Explanation:

https://www.paloaltonetworks.com/documentation/70/pan-os/newfeaturesguide/wildfire-features/wildfire-grayware-verdict

34. Correct Answer: D
35. Correct Answer: A
36. Correct Answer: D
37. Correct Answer: C
38. Correct Answer: CD
39. Correct Answer: A
40. Correct Answer: A
41. Correct Answer: BC
42. Correct Answer: A

Explanation:

(https://live.paloaltonetworks.com/t5/Configuration-Articles/How-to-Configure- GlobalProtect/ta-p/58351)

43. Correct Answer: C
44. Correct Answer: BE

Explanation:

(https://www.paloaltonetworks.com/documentation/60/panorama/panorama_adminguide/se t-up-panorama/set-up-the-m-100-appliance)

45. Correct Answer: B
46. Correct Answer: D
47. Correct Answer: ACE
48. Correct Answer: A
49. Correct Answer: BDE

Explanation:

(https://live.paloaltonetworks.com/t5/Featured-Articles/Getting-Started-Packet-Capture/ta- p/72069)